T0345717

# Space Island

## ACTIVITY BOOK

**2**

# Contents

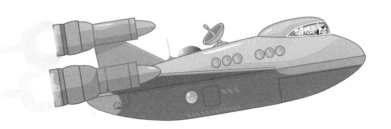

**1** Match.

 **1** ☐ b

 **2** ☐

 **3** ☐

**a** Hello, I'm Professor Bloom.

**b** Hi! I'm Harry. I'm nine.

**c** Hello, my name's Rose.

**2** Draw and write about yourself.

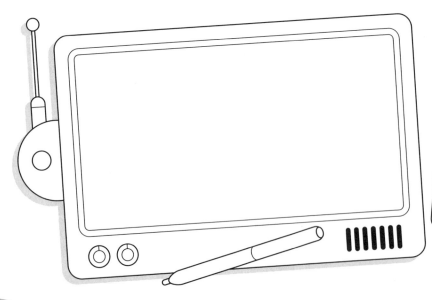

Hello.

My name's _____.

I'm (age) _____.

## 3  Listen, join the dots and write.

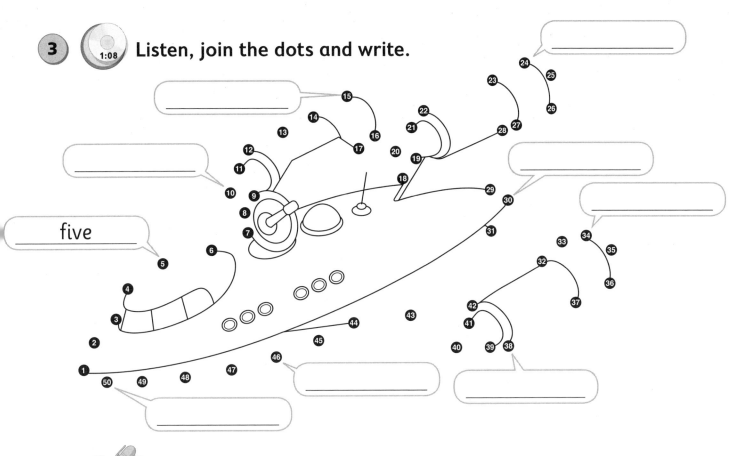

_____

_____

_____

_____

_____ five

_____

_____

_____

_____

## 4 Circle and write the days of the week.

| w | s | t | j | o | a | w | t | m |
|---|---|---|---|---|---|---|---|---|
| m | o | n | d | a | y | e | h | k |
| s | f | t | o | a | b | d | u | l |
| x | w | y | q | o | i | n | r | e |
| s | u | n | d | a | y | e | s | o |
| a | d | f | c | n | m | s | d | y |
| e | b | z | f | r | i | d | a | y |
| s | a | t | u | r | d | a | y | w |
| t | u | e | s | d | a | y | t | v |

Monday

_____

_____

_____

_____

_____

_____

Today is _____. My favourite day is _____.

# 1 Nature

**1** Match.

flowers    insects    birds

pond    rock    animal

**2**  Now colour.

**3** **1:14** **Listen, draw and colour.**

**4** **Look and write.**

**1** __There's__ a blue pond.

**2** __There are__ yellow flowers.

**3** _____ a brown rock.

**4** _____ a purple animal.

**5** _____ pink insects.

**6** _____ blue birds.

**5**  **Write.**

**1** There <u>*are seven*</u> birds.

**2** There _____ mushrooms.

**3** There _____ rocks.

**4** There _____ animals.

**5** There _____ trees.

**6** There _____ clouds.

**7** There _____ pond.

**6**  **Tell the class.**

How many rocks are there?

There are five rocks.

**7**   Look, match and write.

**1** The white horse
**2** Two small birds
**3** The flower and the mushroom

_____    _____

**8** (1:18) Listen and tick (✔).

**1**   ✔

**2**

**3**

**4**

**SOUNDS FUN!**

**9** (1:19) Listen, write and say.

Tr _e_ _e_ s, tr __ __ s, tr __ __ s.        L __ __ s __ __ s.
Gr __ __ n, gr __ __ n, tr __ __ s.         Thr __ __ gr __ __ n tr __ __ s.
Thr __ __ gr __ __ n tr __ __ s.

**10** **Look and correct the mistakes.**

**1** There are two mushrooms.

_There are three mushrooms._

**2** There are two birds.

_____

**3** There's a flower.

_____

**4** There are insects.

_____

**5** There's a rock.

_____

 **11** **Look at the code and write the message.**

H☆ll⚡, H🪐p ⚽nd H⚡p.

a = ⚽
e = ☆
i = 🪐
o = ⚡
u = 🚀

Hello, _____

 **12** **Write a message for your friend in the code.**

_____

**8** **Lesson 5**

**13**  **Draw and write.**

**1**  **+**  **= 6**

**2**  **–**   **= 4**

**3**  **+**  **= 7**

**4**  **–**  **= 2**

**1**  Four insects plus          _____two insects_____ equals six.
**2**  Seven mushrooms minus  _____ equals four.
**3**  Four clouds plus          _____ equals seven.
**4**  Six flowers minus        _____ equals two.

**14**  **Solve the riddle.**

I'm the number of legs on five birds,  _____

Plus the number of legs on two cats.  _____

What number am I?  _____

**15**  **Complete the sums.**

11 + ____ = 13
20 – ____ = 13
12 + ____ = 13
18 – ____ = 13

**16** ✏️ Complete the crossword.

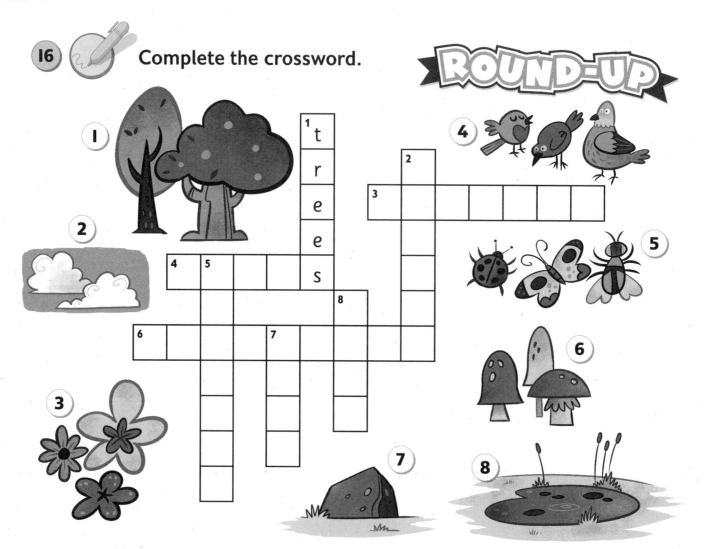

**ROUND-UP**

Across/Down clues numbered 1–8 with pictures:
1 (trees) — **t r e e s**
2 (clouds)
3 (flowers)
4 (birds)
5 (insects)
6 (mushrooms)
7 (rock)
8 (pond)

**17** ✏️ Look and write.

1 There **'s one** tree.

2 There are _____ rocks.

3 There _____ insects.

4 There _____ bird.

5 There _____ clouds.

6 There _____ mushrooms.

7 There _____ flowers.

**18**  Draw and colour your favourite park.

**19** Write about your favourite park.

There's _____

There are _____

**20**  Now tell the class.

Good · Excellent

# 2 Me

**1**  **Listen and colour. Then match.**

Grandad    Mum    Peter

blond hair
red hair
green eyes

Grandad

Mum

Peter

blue eyes
white moustache
small glasses
short beard

**2**  **Write the sentences.**

~~beard~~  blond  green  hair  eyes  small  moustache

**1** Grandad has got a short ___beard___ and a white _____.
He's got _____ eyes and _____ glasses.
**2** Mum's got _____ hair.
**3** Peter's got red _____.
**4** Mum and Peter have got blue _____.

**3**  **Choose, draw and write.**

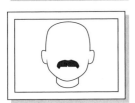
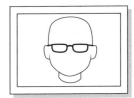

I've got _____

_____

I haven't got _____

**4** **Look and write.**

> He's got    She's got
> He hasn't got    She hasn't got

1  ___He's got___ long hair.    5  ___She's got___ long hair.
2  _____ a moustache.    6  _____ glasses.
3  _____ glasses.    7  _____ a moustache.
4  _____ a beard.    8  _____ a beard.

**5** 1:31 **Listen and draw.**

Have you got big teeth?

Yes, I have.

SONG

Zig

Zog

**6** **Write about the aliens.**

Zog has got _____

Zog hasn't got _____

Zig _____

_____

**7**  Listen, tick (✔) and find the girl.

**1**  ✔

**2**

**3**

Kelly

Laura

Trudie

**8**  Now write about the girl.

| glasses | black |
| nose | She |
| teeth | She's |

She's got short ¹_____black_____ hair.
She's got a small ²_____.
³_____ got big ⁴_____.
⁵_____ hasn't got ⁶_____.
She's ⁷_____!

**9**  Rewrite with capital letters and full stops.

he's got short blond hair

_____

he's got big eyes and a small nose

_____

**10**  Listen and circle the sound that's different.

| 1 | Sharon | (chair) | sheep | 3 | she | ship | they |
| 2 | hair | shoe | shape | 4 | shell | small | short |

**11**  **Look, read and match.**

| 1 | He's got a long neck. | 3 | He's got big teeth. |
| 2 | He's got short hair. | 4 | He's got a big nose. |

**12**  **Draw and write.**

He's got
five eyes, big ears, a
long neck, long hair
and big teeth.

_____

_____

**13** **Look at the code on page 8 and write the message.**

Hꙮp lꙮk☆s Hꙮrry.

_____

**14** Complete the diagram.

| two legs | feathers | long legs | short legs | pouch |
| long tail | wings | short neck | long neck | big ears |

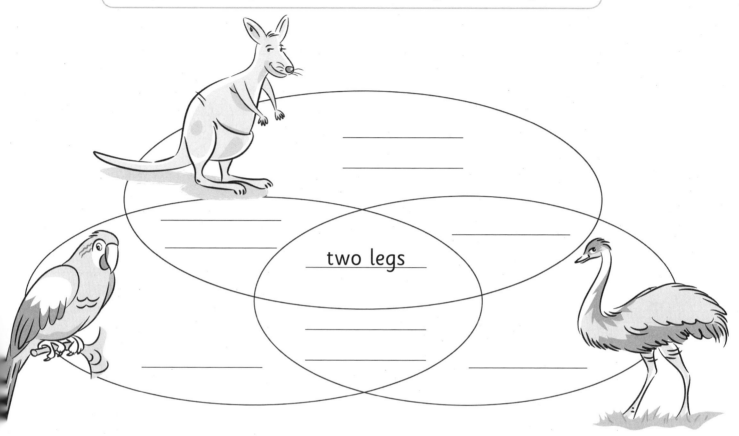

_____
_____

_____
_____

_____
_____

two legs

_____

_____

**15** Invent an animal. Draw and write.

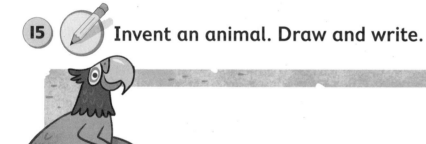

My animal's got _____

My animal hasn't got _____

**16**  **Circle and write the words.**

| t | e | e | t | h | p | s | b | s |
|---|---|---|---|---|---|---|---|---|
| u | m | o | u | s | t | a | e | c |
| g | l | a | s | s | e | s | a | a |
| l | n | o | p | e | m | n | r | r |
| o | s | r | a | c | s | o | d | e |
| p | o | t | a | p | i | s | o | y |
| h | a | i | r | h | e | e | e | e |
| c | a | r | b | n | e | c | k | s |
| m | o | u | s | t | a | c | h | e |

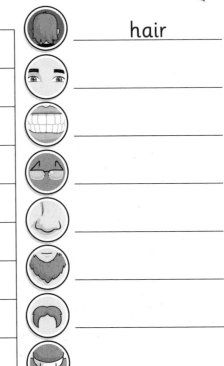

hair
_____

_____

_____

_____

_____

_____

_____

_____

**17** **Read and circle four errors. Then write.**

Kenny

Kenny is a koala. He's got big eyes and small ears. He hasn't got a pouch. He's got feathers and a tail.

Kenny's got _____

He hasn't got _____

**18**  **Draw yourself.**

**19**  **Write about yourself.**

I've got _____ hair and _____ eyes.

I haven't got _____.

**20** **Now tell the class.**

 Good     Excellent

# 3 Pets

**1**  Match.

1 cat · f
2 frog
3 rabbit
4 snake
5 parrot
6 fish

**2** 🔊 1:40 Listen and write.

We've got a ___cat___  and

a _____ . We haven't got a dog.

We've got a _____ ,

a _____ and a _____ .

We haven't got a fish.

**3**  **Look and write.**

**1** Has it got a big mouth? ___Yes, it has.___
Has it got a tail? _____
What is it? It's a _____.

**2** Has it got legs? _____
Has it got two eyes? _____
What is it? It's a _____.

**4**  **Answer the questions.**

**1** Has the cat got wings? _____No, it hasn't._____
**2** Has the dog got two eyes? _____
**3** Has the parrot got four legs? _____
**4** Has the fish got a tail? _____
**5** Has the rabbit got ears? _____
**6** Has the frog got two legs? _____

**5**  **Write a description of an animal.**

This is a _____.It's got _____
and _____ but it hasn't got_____.

**6**  Listen and draw.

**7** Complete the questions. Then answer.

**1** Have the cats got pretty _____noses_____ ( **sosne** )?

**2** Have the tortoises got ugly _____ ( **gels** )?

**3** Have the snakes got _____ eyes ( **tyrept** )?

**4** Have the tortoises got _____ ( **salit** )?

**5** Have the hamsters got ugly _____ ( **hetet** )?

**6** Have the cats got _____ eyes ( **lgyu** )?

**8**  **1:48** **Listen and circle.**

**SKILLS**

**Animal:** fish / (parrot)
**Name:** Luke / Lily
**Home:** Australia / South America
**Age:** 8 years old / 10 years old
**Legs:** 4 legs / 2 legs
**Food:** likes apples / likes insects

**9**   **Read and write.**

> legs   Lily   pretty   eight   ~~parrot~~
> South America   apples   two

Hello, I'm Sophie and I've got a pet. It's a ¹___parrot___. Its name is
²_____ and it's from ³_____. It's ⁴_____ years old.
It hasn't got four ⁵_____, it's got ⁶_____ legs. It's very
⁷_____. It likes ⁸_____.

**SOUNDS FUN!**

**10**  **1:49** **Listen and write the words in the correct column.**

| | | | **bat** | **make** |
|---|---|---|---|---|
| **1** cat | **4** cake | | cat | |
| **2** snake | **5** lake | | | |
| **3** rat | **6** hat | | | |

**Listen and write.**

**STORY**

**1** This animal has got ___four___ legs and long ___ears___. It's a ___rabbit___.

**2** This animal has got _____ and a _____. It's a _____.

**3** This animal has got two _____. It hasn't got _____. It's a _____.

**4** This animal has got fur, a long _____ and four _____. It's a _____.

**12**   **Look at the code on page 8 and write the message.**

Hssplo hos gst glosss.

**13**   **Look and write.**

**Life cycle of a frog**

 1 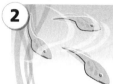 2  3  4

_____eggs_____ _____ _____ _____

**Life cycle of a butterfly**

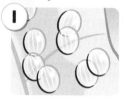 1  2  3  4

_____ _____ _____ _____

eggs
cocoons
butterflies
tadpoles
caterpillars
eggs
frogs
big tadpoles

**14**  **Answer the questions.**

**1** Have butterflies got big mouths?    _____No, they haven't._____
**2** Have frogs got big eyes?    _____
**3** Have big tadpoles got legs?    _____
**4** Have caterpillars got legs?    _____
**5** Have cocoons got eyes?    _____

**15**  **Describe the frog.**

The frog has got _____

_____

**16**  Look and write.

_____ cat _____    _____    _____

_____    _____    _____

_____    _____    _____

**17** (1:53) Listen and tick (✔).

|  | four legs | short tail | big mouth | big eyes | young |
|---|---|---|---|---|---|
| hamster | ✔ |  |  |  |  |
| tortoise |  |  |  |  |  |
| frog |  |  |  |  |  |

**18** Write.

The hamster _____

The tortoise _____

The frog _____

**19** Draw and colour your favourite pet.

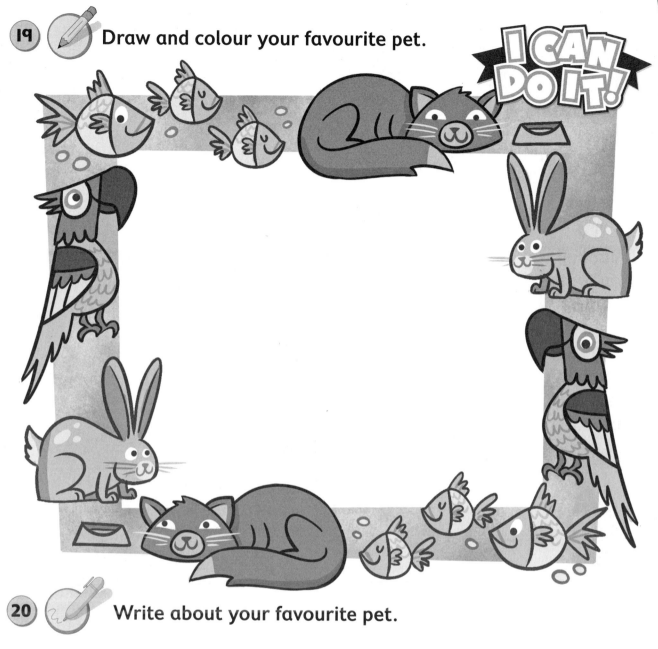

**20** Write about your favourite pet.

My favourite pet is a _____

It's _____

**21** Now tell the class.

Good ⭐ ⭐ ⭐ ⭐ ⭐ Excellent

# 4 Home

**1** Match.

bed
TV
cooker
cupboard
shower
sofa
living room
kitchen
bedroom
bathroom

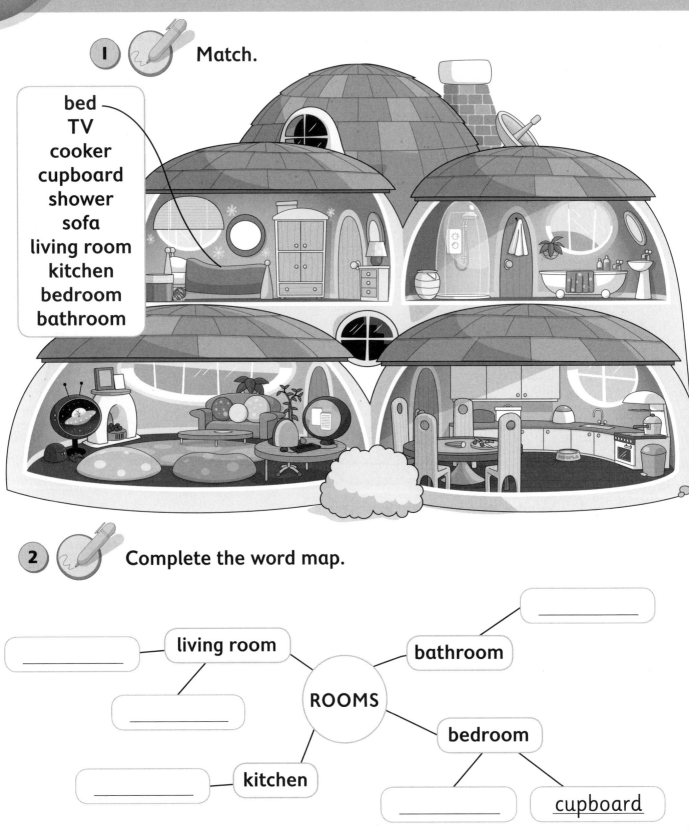

**2** Complete the word map.

living room

_____

_____

_____   kitchen

ROOMS

bathroom

_____

bedroom

_____   <u>cupboard</u>

**1** Is the cooker in the kitchen?  (**Yes, it is.**) / No, it isn't.
**2** Is the sofa in the bedroom?  Yes, it is. / No, it isn't.
**3** Is the shower in the bathroom?  Yes, it is. / No, it isn't.
**4** Is the bed in the living room?  Yes, it is. / No, it isn't.

**4**  **Draw and answer.**

Yes, it is.    No, it isn't.

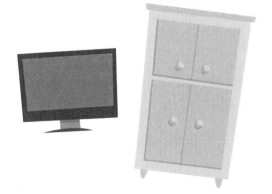

**1** Is the TV in the living room?

_____

**2** Is the cupboard in the bathroom?

_____

**5**   Where's the frog?

on ~~in~~ under

The frog is __in__ the bath.

The frog is _____ the lamp.

The frog is _____ the chair.

**6** 2:07 **Look and answer. Then listen and check.**

**1** Where's the frog?     It's on the bed.

**2** Where's the tortoise? _____

**3** Where's the snake? _____

**4** Where's the hamster? _____

**5** Where's the parrot? _____

**6** Where's the rabbit? _____

**7**  **Listen and write punctuation marks.**

I'm very happy. I've got a great new air chair
It's cool  Where's the chair  In my bedroom
It's fantastic  It's grey and it's got a hamster
on it  Where's the hamster  It's on the ball
The chair is fun  Do you like it

**SOUNDS FUN!**

**8**  **Listen and circle the sound that's different.**

| | | | |
|---|---|---|---|
| **1** | hot | dog | (school) |
| **2** | cool | frog | pool |
| **3** | frog | cool | dog |
| **4** | school | pool | hot |

**q** Look and complete.

| in | on | under | | shower | lamp | sofa | pond | bed | chair |

**1** The hamster is ___in___ the __shower__.

**2** The hamster is _____ the _____.

**3** The hamster is _____ the _____.

**4** The hamster is _____ the _____.

**5** The hamster is _____ the _____.

**6** The hamster is _____ the _____.

 **10** Look at the code on page 8 and write the message.

H⦵p's g⚡t  p☆t h⦵mst☆r.

_____

  **Draw the next four shapes on the frame.
Then colour.**

**12** **Write the words. Then draw a mosaic animal.**

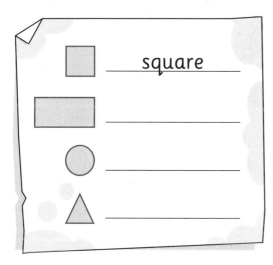

square

**13** **Count, answer and write.**

**1** How many triangles
are there?

**3** How many squares
are there?

**2** How many circles
are there?

**4** How many rectangles
are there?

This is my mosaic animal. It's got _____ squares. It's got _____

_____

**14**  **Think and write the words.**

1  kecoor ___cooker___    4  thab _____

2  bupodcar _____    5  plam _____

3  wosher _____    6 hcari _____

**15** **Read and draw. Then write.**

bedroom                 bathroom

The cooker and the chair
are in the kitchen. There
is a frog under the chair.
The TV, the sofa and
the lamp are in the living
room. The lamp is on
the table. The bath and
the shower are in the
bathroom. The bed and
the cupboard are in the
bedroom. There are books
under the bed.

kitchen                 living room

1   The cooker and the chair are _____in_____ the kitchen.
2   The frog is _____ the chair.
3   The lamp is _____ the table.
4   The bath and shower are _____ the bathroom.
5   The bed is _____ the bedroom.
6   There are books _____ the bed.

**16**  **Draw and colour your bedroom.**

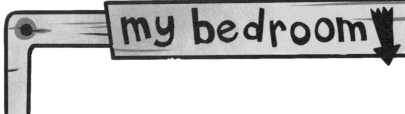

my bedroom

**17**  **Write about your bedroom.**

My favourite room is my bedroom. It's got a bed, a cupboard, a table and a lamp. There are books in the cupboard. The lamp is on the table.

My bedroom has got _____

_____

There are _____

_____

**18**  **Now tell the class.**

Good ☆ ☆ ☆ ☆ ☆ Excellent

# 5 Clothes

**1** Match.

| | |
|---|---|
| **a** | trainers |
| **b** | shirt |
| **c** | jeans |
| **d** | hat |
| **e** | shorts |
| **f** | tracksuit |
| **g** | sweatshirt |

**2** 2:18 Listen and tick (✓). Then write.

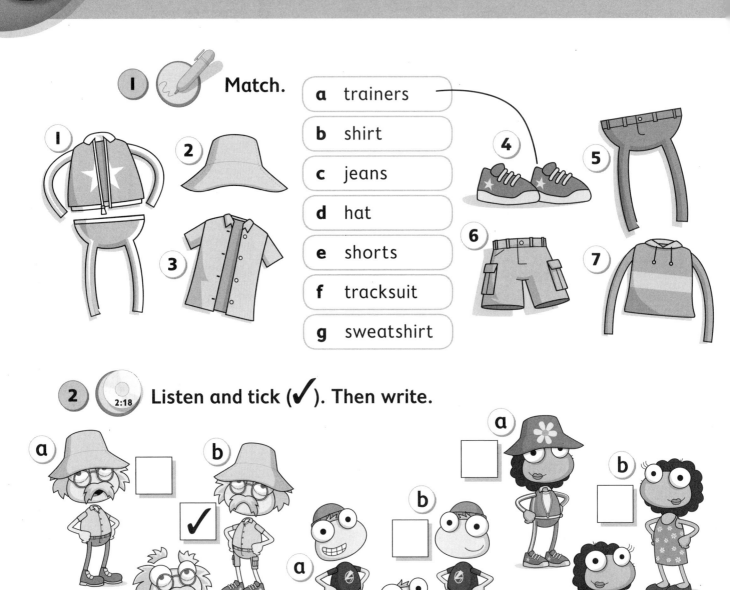

**1** I'm wearing a _____, _____, _____ and a _____.

**2** I'm wearing _____, _____ and a _____.

**3** I'm _____ a _____, a _____, _____ and a _____.

**3**  **Listen and draw. Then colour.**

What are you wearing, Harry?

**4** **Now write about Harry.**

Harry's wearing _____, a _____,
_____ and a _____.

**5**  Listen and colour.

**6**  Read and answer.

> Yes, he/she is.    No, he/she isn't.

| | | |
|---|---|---|
| **1** | Is he wearing blue jeans? | Yes, he is. |
| **2** | Is he wearing yellow trainers? | |
| **3** | Is he wearing a blue T-shirt? | |
| **4** | Is she wearing a brown coat? | |
| **5** | Is she wearing a red scarf? | |
| **6** | Is she wearing pink shoes? | |
| **7** | Is she wearing blue socks? | |

**7**  **Listen and tick (✔).**

| big shoes | ☐ |

| small shoes | ☐ |

| big hat | ☐ |

| small hat | ☐ |

| short skirt | ☐ |

| long skirt | ☐ |

| big shirt | ☐ |

| small shirt | ✔ |

**8**  **What is Hilda wearing? Write.**

Hilda is wearing _____

This is her favourite _____

These are her favourite _____

**9**  **Listen and write. Then put the words in the correct column.**

| | | | *sh* | *sk* |
|---|---|---|---|---|
| **1** | hotsr | ___short___ | **sh**ort | |
| **2** | ysk | _____ | _____ | _____ |
| **3** | woerhs | _____ | _____ | _____ |
| **4** | pikpers | _____ | | |
| **5** | thirs | _____ | | |
| **6** | rsikt | _____ | | |

 **10** Read and circle five errors. Then write.

Harry is wearing his favourite hat and a T-shirt. Hop's wearing a long skirt and his favourite trainers. Rose is wearing shorts. Hoopla is wearing glasses and a hat!

_____

_____

_____

**11** (2:30) Listen, colour and write.

Hip is wearing a _____ and _____ . She's wearing _____ trainers.

Rose is wearing an _____ , a _____ sweatshirt and a _____ skirt. She's wearing _____ .

**12** Look at the code on page 8 and write the message.

Hp s wrng  ht.

_____

**13** Tick (✔) the chores you like.

lay the table

wash the dishes

make the bed

wash the car

tidy up the bedroom

make a cake

 **14** Write your chore list.

| Monday | lay the table |
| Tuesday | |
| Wednesday | |

| Thursday | |
| Friday | |

**15** Circle and write the words.

**What are you wearing?**

| s | g | z | u | o | s | t | e | k | s |
|---|---|---|---|---|---|---|---|---|---|
| w | c | s | s | c | a | r | f | j | h |
| e | c | h | l | d | c | a | z | i | o |
| a | c | i | t | c | l | i | j | i | r |
| t | f | r | y | o | j | n | e | o | t |
| s | a | t | h | a | s | e | a | e | s |
| h | a | t | d | t | o | r | n | e | w |
| i | f | e | u | z | c | s | s | q | e |
| r | t | r | a | c | k | s | u | i | t |
| t | s | h | o | e | s | b | v | q | n |

trainers

_____

_____

_____

_____

_____

_____

_____

_____

**16** Correct the sentences.

**1** He is wearing a sweatshirt.
   He is wearing a T-shirt.

**2** He is wearing trousers.

**3** He is wearing shoes.

**42**   **Round-up**

**17** Draw and colour your favourite clothes.

**18** Write about your favourite clothes.

This is my favourite _____

These are my favourite _____

**19** Now tell the class.

Good ☆ ☆ ☆ ☆ Excellent

# 6 Sports

**1**  **Match and say.**

**a** ride a bike  **b** play football  **c** run
**d** play tennis  **e** jump  **f** swim

c

**2**  **Read and circle.**

jumprunrideabikeswimplayfootballplaytennis

44 **Lesson 1**

**3** 🔊 2:39 **Listen and tick (✔) or cross (✗).**

| |  running | cycling | jumping | swimming | tennis | football |
|---|---|---|---|---|---|---|
| Prof. Bloom | | | | ✔ | | |
| Rose | | | | | | |
| Hip | | | | | | |
| Hop | | | | | | |
| Harry | | | | | | |

**4** ✏️ **Write.**

**1** I <u>can't</u> jump but I _____ swim.

**2** I _____ play tennis but I _____ play football.

**3** I _____ run but I _____ swim.

**4** I _____ play tennis and I _____ jump.

**5** I _____ play football but I _____ ride a bike.

**5**  **Listen and tick (✔) or cross (✗).**

**6**  **Complete.**

1 Can she _____? Yes, she can.
2 Can he _____? No, he can't.
3 Can she play tennis? _____
4 Can he jump? _____

**46    Lesson 3**

**7**  **Listen and tick (✔)** *can* **or cross (✗)** *can't.*

**8**  **Write** *and* **or** *but.*

Monkeys can run ¹ <u>and</u> jump ² _____ they can't ride a bike. They can swim ³ _____ climb trees ⁴ _____ they can't play tennis. They can catch a ball ⁵ _____ they can't play football.

**9** **Listen and write the words in the correct column.**

| k | c |
|---|---|
| mon**k**ey | |
| | |
| | |
| | |

**10**   **Listen and number.**

**a**

**b**   1

**c**

**d**

**11**  **Look, colour and write.**

Hi, I'm Jax. I've got short, brown  _____.

I'm wearing a yellow  _____ and blue

_____. I love  _____. Look at

my _____. It's orange and white. It's got

long  _____ and pretty _____.

It's my new pet! Thank you, Professor Bloom!

**12**  **Look at the code on page 8 and write the message.**

H⚡⚡pl⊙ c⊙n cl⊙mb ⊙ tr⭐⭐ b⚡t h⭐ c⊙n't sw⊙m

**13** 2:49 **Listen and number the pictures.**

PE

[ ] [ ] [ ] [ ] 1

**14** **Make an exercise plan.**

| climb trees | play tennis |
| play football | run | ~~dance~~ |
| swim | ride my bike |
| jump | play basketball |

**My exercise plan**

| Monday | dance |
|---|---|
| Tuesday | |
| Wednesday | |
| Thursday | |

| Friday | |
|---|---|
| Saturday | |
| Sunday | |

**15** **Write about your exercise plan.**

On Monday, I can dance. On Tuesday, _____

_____

_____

_____

**16**  Match.

| 1 | play tennis | 3 | ride a bike | 5 | climb trees | 7 | play football |
|---|---|---|---|---|---|---|---|
| 2 | run | 4 | jump | 6 | swim | 8 | play basketball |

Ted

Sue

Lee

Liz

**17**  Look and write.

1 Ted ___can swim but he can't ride a bike.___

2 Sue _____

3 Lee _____

4 Liz _____

**18** 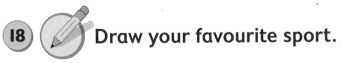 Draw your favourite sport.

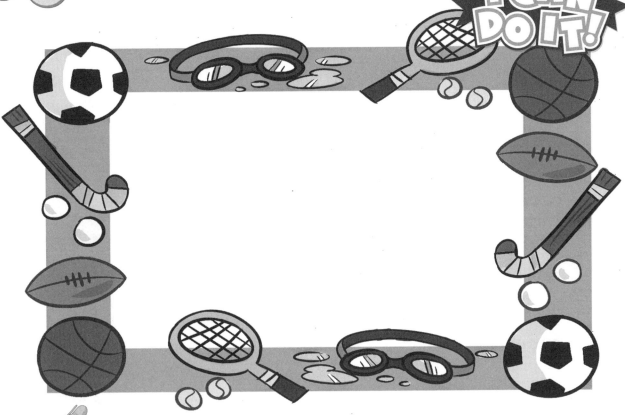

**19** Write about your favourite sport.

My favourite sport is basketball. I can run, jump and catch a ball.

My favourite sport is _____

I can _____

**20** Now tell the class.

# 7 Food

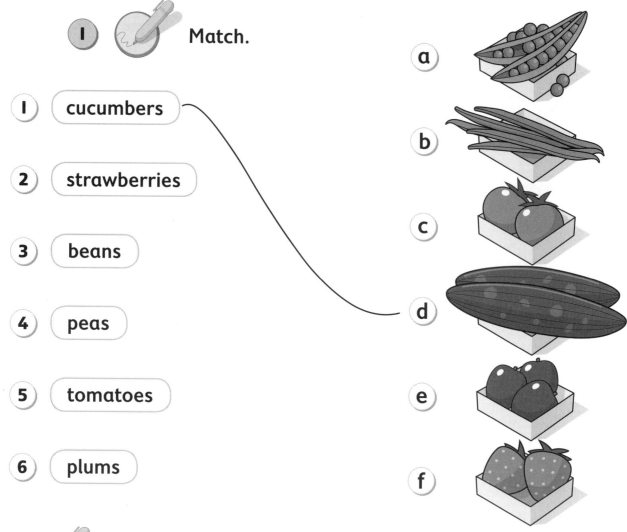

**1** ✎ Match.

1. cucumbers
2. strawberries
3. beans
4. peas
5. tomatoes
6. plums

a

b

c

d

e

f

**2** ✎ Write about the food you like.

☺ I like _____

_____

☹ I don't like _____

_____

**3** 3:06 **Listen and tick (✔) or cross (✗).**

**4** **Now write *likes* or *doesn't like*.**

**1** She _____likes_____ strawberries.
**2** She _____ plums.
**3** She _____ peas.

**4** He _____ cucumbers.
**5** He _____ beans.
**6** He _____ tomatoes.

 **5** Look and answer.

| Does he/she like . . . | Tim | Liz |
|---|---|---|
| peaches? | ✓ | ✓ |
| potatoes? | ✓ | ✗ |
| cucumbers? | ✗ | ✓ |
| carrots? | ✗ | ✗ |
| beans? | ✗ | ✗ |
| plums? | ✓ | ✓ |
| strawberries? | ✓ | ✗ |
| peas? | ✗ | ✓ |

**1** Does Tim like beans?        No, he doesn't.

**2** Does he like potatoes?        _____

**3** Does he like cucumbers?        _____

**4** Does Liz like peaches?        _____

**5** Does she like carrots?        _____

**6** Does she like strawberries?        _____

 **6** Write about Tim and Liz.

Tim likes _____

He doesn't like _____

Liz likes _____

She doesn't like _____

**7**  Listen and draw a happy or sad face.

**8** Look and write.

1  Does he like cereal?     Yes, he does.
2  Does he like strawberries?  _____
3  Does he like eggs and toast?  _____
4  Does he like peaches?  _____
5  _____ bananas?   Yes, he does.
6  _____ plums?   No, he doesn't.

**SOUNDS FUN!**

**9**  Listen and write *p* or *b*.

1  [  ]   2  [  ]   3  CEREAL [  ]   4  [  ]

5  [  ]   6  [  ]   7  [  ]   8  [  ]

 **Look and write the questions and answers.**

**1**

Does he like plums?
Yes, he does.

**2**

_____

_____

**3**

_____

_____

**4**

_____

_____

**5**

_____

_____

**6**

_____

_____

**11**  **Look at the code on page 8 and write the message.**

Pr✪f☆ss✪r Bl⚡⚡m l✪k☆s ◯c☆ cr☆⚽m t⚡⚡!

_____

**12**  Choose and write five healthy snacks.

**13** Draw three healthy meals. Use food from the food pyramid.

breakfast

lunch

dinner

**14** Now write about your three healthy meals.

For breakfast, I like _____

For lunch, I like _____

For dinner, I like _____

**15** Complete the crossword.

ROUND-UP

1  p l u m s

What word can you find?  p _ _ _ _ _ _ _ _

**16**  Look and answer.

1  Does he like beans?          Yes, he does.
2  Does he like carrots?        _____
3  Does he like potatoes?       _____
4  Does he like peas?           _____

**17**  Write.

He likes _____

He doesn't like _____

**18**  Draw your favourite food.

**19** Now write about your favourite food.

I like apples. Big, red apples. They're sweet and nice. They are good for me. Yum!

I like _____

_____

**20**  Now tell the class.

Good  Excellent

# 8 Things we do

**1**  **Match the pictures with the words.**

**a** eating
**b** reading
**c** sleeping
**d** cleaning
**e** drinking
**f** making a rocket

**2** (3:17) **Listen and number the sentences.**

I'm sleeping on the chair. ☐    I'm reading. ☐

I'm drinking water. ☐    I'm eating a sandwich. ☐ 1

I'm making a rocket. ☐    I'm cleaning. ☐

**3** 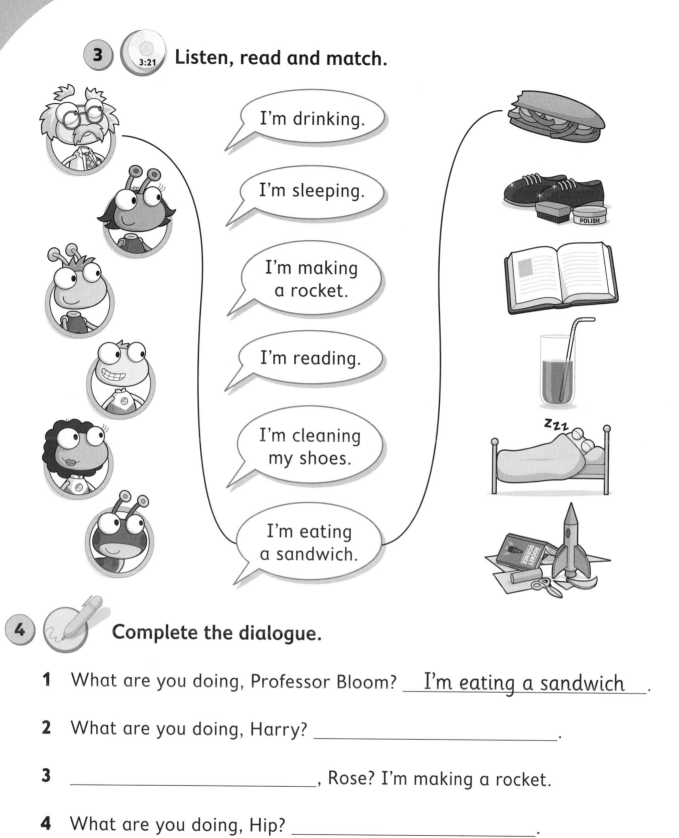 Listen, read and match.

I'm drinking.

I'm sleeping.

I'm making a rocket.

I'm reading.

I'm cleaning my shoes.

I'm eating a sandwich.

**4** Complete the dialogue.

**1** What are you doing, Professor Bloom? __I'm eating a sandwich__ .

**2** What are you doing, Harry? _____.

**3** _____, Rose? I'm making a rocket.

**4** What are you doing, Hip? _____.

**5** _____, Hop? _____.

**6** What is Hoopla doing? _____.

**5**  Listen and tick (✔) or cross (✗).

**SONG**

1 ✔

2 ☐

3 ☐

4 ☐

5 ☐

6 ☐

 **6** Write the questions. Then answer.

Yes, I am.   No, I'm not.

1 ( you ) ( Are ) ( jumping )   _Are you jumping?_   _Yes, I am._

2 ( running ) ( Are ) ( you )   _____   _____

3 ( you ) ( walking ) ( Are )   _____   _____

4 ( swimming ) ( you ) ( Are )   _____   _____

5 ( Are ) ( sleeping ) ( you )   _____   _____

6 ( you ) ( drinking ) ( Are )   _____   _____

**7** 3:26 **Listen and complete the postcard.**

Hi . . .
I'm in Spain, at the beach. It's great
and it's hot! I'm ¹ ___eating___
a ² _____ by the pool.
My sister is ³ _____
and Mum ⁴ _____ ⁵ _____ .
See you soon!
Bye,
Adam

To: _____

_____

_____

_____

_____

3:27 **Now listen and write the address.**

10 Hill Street
W1G 9DQ
Mr and Mrs Smith
England
London

**SOUNDS FUN!**

**8** 3:28 **Listen and match.**

1

2

3

a ( reading )

b ( walking )

c ( sleeping )

d ( eating )

e ( drinking )

f ( swimming )

4

5

6

**9** Look and complete.

| drinking | ~~eating~~ | ball | reading | catching | sandwich | machines |
|---|---|---|---|---|---|---|

> Hi, Harry. What are you doing?

Hi, Hip. I'm ¹___eating___ a ²_____. Rose is ³_____
and Professor Bloom is ⁴_____ about ⁵_____. Oh, and my
dog's ⁶_____ a ⁷_____. What are you doing?

**10** **3:30** Look and write. Then listen and check.

| making a cake |
|---|
| cleaning    sleeping |

> Hi Harry. I'm _____
>
> _____
>
> _____

**11** Look at the code on page 8 and write the message.

H⚽rry ⚽nd R⚡s☆ ⚽r☆ h⚡m☆ ⚡n ☆⚽rth.

_____

**12**  **3:32** **Listen and draw.**

 **13** **Now write about your flying machine.**

pilot   wings   glasses   round   **ATLAS**   tails

This is a new flying machine.
It's big and _____.
It's got four _____ and two _____.
The name is _____.
It's got a _____.
He's wearing big _____.

**14** Complete the crossword.

| 1 | s | w | i | m | m | i | n | g |
|---|---|---|---|---|---|---|---|---|

1
2
3

4
5

What word can you find?   s _ _ _ _ _ _ _ _ _

**15** Complete the sentences.

running   jumping   swimming   walking

**What are you doing?**

I'm running.

66   Round-up

**16**   **Draw your favourite activity.**

**17**  **Write about your picture.**

I'm _____

_____

**18**  **Now tell the class.**

Good ★ ★ ★ ★ ★ Excellent

# Christmas

**1** Find the words. Then match.

**1** gctoiskns
   _stockings_

**2** srmtshCia   erte

   _____

**3** sarcd

   _____

**4** antSa

   _____

**5** siglht

   _____

**6** nepstres

   _____

**2**  Listen, draw and colour. Then write.

I've got a lot of Christmas presents. I've got a _____

_____

# Easter

**1** Look and write.

_____  _____  _____  _____

**2** 3:41 Find the Easter eggs. Listen, draw and colour.

**3** Now write and match.

> pink   yellow   green   blue   red   purple

1  __The blue egg is__ — in the
2  _____ on the
3  _____ under the
4  _____ in the
5  _____ on the
6  _____ under the

# Picture dictionary

## Nature

flowers

rock

pond

birds

animal

insects

mushrooms

trees

clouds

## Me

eyes

long hair

glasses

short hair

beard

moustache

nose

neck

teeth

## Animals

cat

frog

fish

rabbit

parrot

snake

dog

tortoise

hamster

# Home

TV

cooker

cupboard

bed

shower

sofa

bath

chair

lamp

# Clothes

trainers

shirt

jeans

hat

tracksuit

shorts

sweatshirt

scarf

coat

# Sports

run

ride a bike

play tennis

jump

swim

play football

play basketball

catch a ball

climb a tree

# Food

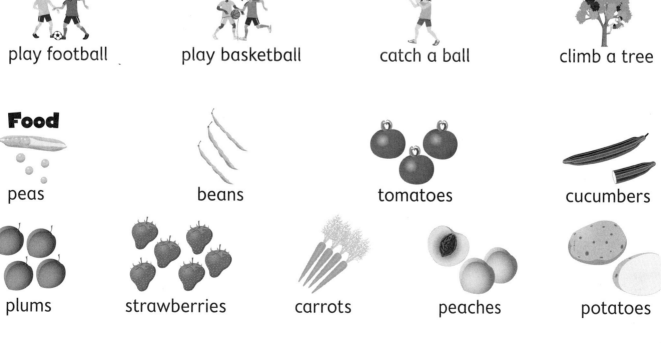

peas

beans

tomatoes

cucumbers

plums

strawberries

carrots

peaches

potatoes

# Things we do

sleeping

reading

eating

drinking

cleaning

making a rocket

jumping

swimming

# Christmas

Santa

Christmas tree

cards

lights

stockings

presents

# Easter

Easter bunny

Easter basket

ribbon

Easter egg